Ancient Wisdom for Modern Times

30 DAYS

—— *with the* ——

SAGES

Heal Your Soul by Changing Your Thinking

CAROL CURRIER

30 Days with the Sages

Copyright © 2022

Published by Elevate Publishing

ISBN 979-8-9862830-6-7 (paperback)

Printed in the United States of America

To my teachers and my students and
especially to David and Chana and their daughters.

Contents

The images throughout the book are symbols of truths the sages would have recognized. The palm tree is like a righteous person whose life is fruitful and fulfilling even in old age. Sheep bring us sustenance but require guidance and protection. Each symbol emphasizes a truth.

Introduction

There are few times in history when wise ones clustered in close villages, teaching and correcting one another. The times of Pirke Avot* (The Saying of the Fathers) was such an era. They had all memorized the foundational teaching of Lady Wisdom and could weave these ideas in and out of any conversation. Somehow, we have the merit to learn from brief chapters of their ideas.

We are not such an era. We don't revere the wise; we criticize and tear down teachers. But we can use the words of the wise and their paradoxical sayings to sit at their feet.

This book is about using words of the sages to gain perspective on how we are living.

Really, any benefit you gain from this book is up to you. I am not a scholar. I am simply a seeker of wisdom. But I offer you these thoughts with wholehearted love and respect.

*I have used the translation "Pirke Avot" by Joseph I. Gorfinkle, PhD.

DAY

1

Do not say, "When I have leisure, I will study."

—Hillel 2:5

There is an amazing ability to get things done when you don't wait for the "right time." In many ways, desire causes energy.

For example, Joe arrives home exhausted after work, collapsing into his recliner. Then there's a knock at the door, and Bill and Matt are there. "Hey, Joe, we're going to get pizza. Want to come?" "Sure!" He desires fun and being with his buddies, and pizza sounds good. He is up and about.

Desire ignites energy. The desire to study can be cultivated. Even a tiny spark of desire can be turned into the flame of a burning desire. How do we uncover a spark of desire and cultivate it into a flame? We can ask ourselves the question:

"What would I love to be, do, or have?"

Let me share a little secret about myself. Today, as for many decades, when waking up, my first thought is: "I want wisdom!" Sometimes, it's like a prayer to the Creator. "More than my next breath of air, I desire wisdom." Sometimes I think, "Maybe there are others who could be wise, but they don't care. I care. Any wisdom lying around unclaimed, I claim today!" I think maybe I missed a lesson of wisdom yesterday; then I beg for it again today. I tell my dog, the wall, the early morning birds that I am that person who desires wisdom.

Finding a desire, repeating that desire, paying attention to that desire—this is one way to turn a spark into a flame. Going through this process as the last thing at night and/or the first thing in the morning multiplies the intensity of the flame.

Since energy follows desire, if you cultivate the desire to study, you will get yourself to study every day. This process is not primarily about "willpower." It's about cultivating a desire, and the energy will follow. It's about taking a step consistent with the person living the life you desire.

Carol Currier

DAY
2

Despise not any man
and despise not any
thing, for every man
has his time and every
thing has its place.

W/e do live in an era when people may be publicly despised and things may be discarded thoughtlessly. However, there is a beautiful order hidden in the idea that each person has a time that belongs to them, when that life will shine. There is a proper place for everything even if it's just a trash can. Understanding this can give us patience with an unskillful loved one who has not come into their time. Awareness of this truth can organize our space with a sparse, elegant simplicity. Everything has its place.

This understanding is especially valuable applied to our own lives! There is a time for us, and we can prepare for and grow into our time.

This truth has helped me overcome what might be considered setbacks or failures, but these experiences are just preparation for my mastery when it is my time.

And I have seen it in others, professionally and personally. How many times have you heard of others whose final decade of career is their time of greatest contribution or the person who marries the love of their life in their 60s?

We all are diamonds in the rough. Give us the wisdom to treasure people and things even before their time has beauty come.

DAY
3

Be the first to greet.

When we see someone coming toward us, we can recognize the Light in that person and affirm it by greeting them immediately. Ego can find may excuses to wait for someone else to greet us, but in the end, it amounts to a blindness toward human dignity.

Every person is valuable beyond measure. It may not be apparent at the moment, but it is true anyhow. When we look past circumstances to see this truth, we also affirm the best in ourselves. I like to tell myself that my greeting will make the other person's day better.

DAY

4

The wise man does not
speak before someone
with greater wisdom.

Sadly, I have a tendency to be impulsive in speech, to feel I am bursting with ideas I want to share. Restricting myself on this one issue has resulted in some of the best insights I have ever heard. By letting the decision to listen first control my thoughts, I can recognize those around me who have greater wisdom. Of course, there are many situations I go into already knowing another person has greater wisdom. I have a friend who is a skilled therapist, and decades have gone into distilling the wisdom of those therapy techniques. Why would I speak first? I have a friend who is a skilled nutritionist. We are looking over the menu. Why would I speak first?

Many people wait for a pause before they speak. You can tell them with your eyes that you are listening.

DAY
5

The wise person
does not interrupt
his companions.

F amilies have their customs. In my family, we were passion-
ate about ideas, and we all spoke at once. Somehow, we all
heard and understood one another. It was only in adult-
hood that I learned that all social situations are not like this.
Some people may resent being interrupted, or some may just go
silent and back off, no longer contributing. Frequently, if I wait,
I find out the end of a sentence has a different meaning than
the beginning, so it is worth waiting. I sometimes count three
beats in my head and say, "Tell me more about that." Because,
guess what? I didn't fully understand the point they were making. Generally, I already know any insight I might want to share,
but I don't know what my friend will share.

DAY
6

A wise person is not
hasty to answer.

W hen I was in school, I was so eager to answer that I was formulating a response before the question was finished. Of course, there were plenty of tests when I got the answer wrong, yet that didn't dim my enthusiasm.

As I've gotten older, I've gotten a little more patient. I like to test the answer mentally now before I speak. I say to myself, "Okay, that's one idea. Is there any other way to look at this?"

Another powerful aspect of this is pausing before making comments. It's too easy to agree to a comment before assessing the cost. How many casual agreements are made without checking the calendar or asking, "Is this really for me?" That casual commitment leaves you left unfulfilled and leads to a lack of trust in relationships and a lack of confidence in your own words. Sad to say, trust is slower to build than to tear down. Our confidence in our own words builds our self-esteem, and few people perform beyond their own self-esteem.

Keeping promises is essential to building self-esteem. Better to not promise than to promise and break that promise.

DAY

7

The wise man questions
according to the
subject matter.

S ome subjects are heavy, and some are light. There is room to hear out our friend's thoughts about a "trivial matter," and there is room to question compassionately at the time of loss and pain.

In addition, some subjects are dangerous. Ascribing negative motives to others can lead us down a very dark path. Perhaps we can inquire if there might be some hidden good or some other viewpoint. When the subject is negative, our questions need to lead us back to the positive. Then, can we harvest the good out of this? Years ago, a friend of mine told me, "Even a mule will eat the hay and leave the briars." Why let the subject of the communication drift to what you don't want? Of course, to practice this takes awareness. My mother used to say that, at birth, we were each given a sack of gold coins. Every coin represented a word we would say in our lifetime. The good words stayed gold, and other words which were not good became wood. When we got ready to leave this world and go to the world to come, everything in the sack was set on fire, and all that was left were the gold ones.

Another dangerous subject is doubt and fear. Some people have rehearsed that negative view so much that they have a script or even a rant that starts up. Listening to this is not beneficial, and nothing good comes of going down that path. It takes skill to move away from that subject. If at all possible, change the subject. If that's not feasible, escape! Realize you have to be somewhere. Arrange to continue the conversation another time. You cannot afford to throw away one minute of your life.

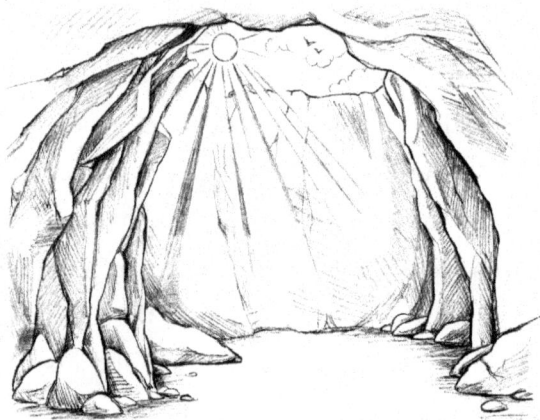

Carol Currier

DAY
8

The wise person
answers to the point.

How many conversations are disconnected? Someone asked a question, and the answer misses the point. Part of this is hearing without listening and part of this is mental laziness resulting in rambling answers. Part of this is spiritual laziness resulting from not looking into the heart of the person speaking. What is their real question? Is there a question behind the question? Sometimes the question is: "Do you care about me? Am I important? I am feeling insecure. Do you believe in me?" Some answers miss the point because of blindness. The listener does not really see the person asking the question. Sometimes it's necessary to ask what's really going on. Is there a feeling I'm getting that is separate or disconnected from the words I just heard? Some questions are just saying, "Look at me." In those cases, it's so important to acknowledge the person first. The real point is that person's dignity.

DAY
9

The wise person speaks
upon the first thing
first and the last, last.

erhaps an ordered mind leads to ordered speech. In any case, disordered speech brings confusion and can result in the listener's mind starting to wander. Economy of speech requires topic one, answer one, topic two, answer two. When the speech is disordered, the listener may think, "What did I just hear?" By keeping the answer in order, we avoid skipping important parts. If parts are skipped due to disorder, even an attentive listener may not notice that several things are missing.

Sometimes when a person is feeling especially clever, the answer becomes very convoluted because too much is being addressed. The answer wears out the listener, and the mind "checks out." The golden moment of wholehearted attention is gone. Communication is not what we said but what the listener heard. In a deeper sense, communication is the action the listener takes!

DAY
10

A wise man regarding that which he has not understood says, "I have not understood it."

t takes wisdom to know when you don't understand. It takes even more wisdom to say you don't understand. One aspect of maturity is to know what you don't know. Another aspect is to exercise humility. All of us can choose to be honest with ourselves about the limits of knowledge and our own understanding. A handy snapshot of our understanding is our stability on a path of good behavior. How stable is your good behavior? If you are irritable with your friends when you are tired, your stability in the behavior of good friendship is low and your understanding is lower. The picture of wisdom in Job 28:28—"See! Fear of the Lord is wisdom; to shun evil is understanding"—is helpful here. Areas where we continue in fruitless behavior are areas where we lack understanding. Open your eyes, and choose to see. "To depart from evil, that is understanding." It doesn't take a lot of brains to choose to be humble. After all, we've all made a few mistakes in our day and have much to be humble about. Humility is actual openness to being taught. The wise person is surely a lifelong learner.

DAY
11

The wise person
acknowledges the truth.

Sometimes it's difficult to say, "I was wrong." Sometimes it's difficult to say, "You were right. I want to apologize." When we are really curious about the truth, the truth will make itself known. It is when we acknowledge the truth that we become responsible for it in our behavior. Once we have really seen the truth, we can't un-see it. Nor can we be at peace pretending we did not see it. By acknowledging the truth, we keep our own self-respect and the respect of those we influence. The problem is not having made a mistake but refusing to admit it. An essential quality of wisdom is a hunger for truth. There is a cost for truth. It is not always easy to recognize truth when it seems uncomfortable. As soon as we recognize truth and acknowledge it, we become able to take action on the basis of that truth. By this process, we develop a resistance to deception.

There is insight in the phrase "He's only kidding himself." Delay in that acknowledgment of truth is the space for self-deception. What is the price of deception? Disconnection. We disconnect from ourselves and others. Estranged, truth treats us as strangers.

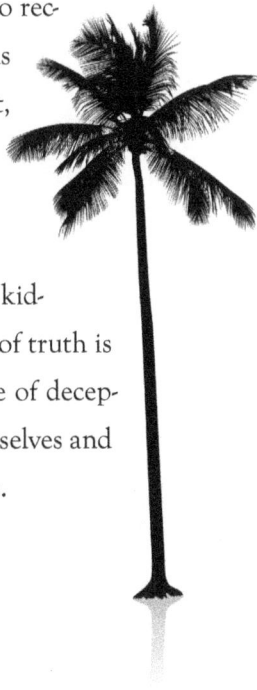

DAY
12

Turn it, and turn it over again for everything is in it.

houghts that are selfish or foolish might come to us despite years of effort. So, in my view, the wisdom of the sages is like the surface of an iceberg: what you see rests on a huge unseen foundation under the water. In many cases, the surface is like old ice; even on a cloudy day, it glows with a turquoise light. It seems that we see it, but then it rotates and a whole new surface with different angles and aspects comes into view.

To turn it, turn it requires patience. There is a great advantage in the practice of some communities that review the same text over and over. In our community, we review the Torah portion every week, and we have a cycle of yearly repetition. Many communities have similar practices. Revisiting the truth revises what you thought you knew. Truth bears repetition. To turn it, turn it is part of the process of learning truth.

DAY
13

Seek not greatness for thyself and court not honor; let thy works exceed thy learning.

Wanting honor implies a need for external affirmation, and knowing more than we practice implies not putting our knowledge to good use. Both of these are attributes of lack of thought. The thoughtful person understands that no amount of external acknowledgement is enough. As much as others might love and respect us, it cannot make up for a hollow feeling inside. Similarly, we may feel very advanced in our learning, but we may have not "proved it" in the laboratory of our own lives. How can we advocate this learning to anyone else? How do we know it works if we never tried it out ourselves?

DAY
14

He who learns from
his companion a single
chapter, a simple
rule, a single verse,
or single expression,
or even a letter ought
to pay him honor.

Thi passage goes on to say David only learned two things from Ahitophel yet regarded him as his master, his guide. Now those of us who are aware of the details of Ahitophel's life and death may not comprehend why David honored Ahitophel. Our honor depends on our greatness, not our weakness. David's great merit was to value the good he gained from Ahitophel. There are many people we owe. We stand on the shoulders of our lineage. We would not be where we are if our teachers did not have teachers. We benefit from everyone that poured good into our lives, even if it did not seem so at the time. We benefit from a light that lit up for us when we heard that comment. That comment is worthy of honor. Some of my most valuable insights came from moments that did not seem valuable at the time but that I valued upon reflection.

DAY
15

Make a fence about truth.

t is fascinating that seasoned teachers and tradition advise us to make a margin of error around our practice of truth. Factor in your weakness. If you need to study 2 hours in the morning to master material, get up 2.5 or 3 hours early. If it takes you 0.5 hours to read the material, allow for 45 minutes and read it out loud with emotion. Why do we light candles on Friday night 18 minutes before sunset in our community? Because we have no intention of encroaching upon what is sacred. For example, similarly, when dealing with wisdom, we make room for extra study. We don't assume we know until we put it in practice.

DAY
16

The world rests upon
three things . . . acts
of loving kindness.

t is easy to see how the stability of our world might be based on the truth (Torah) and on work in service of truth (avodah), but acts of loving kindness? Truth and work seem weightier than acts of loving kindness, which could really be a small gesture for some unknown person. Any person could do an act of loving kindness. There are barriers and qualifications for the first two, but the third only requires a kindness of vision and heart. The decision to help is often spontaneous, without preparation. In fact, if we overthink it, the moment for action may pass and be out of our reach. Being a person who habitually performs acts of loving kindness requires an advance decision to be that person and a willingness to walk around noticing others and stepping in to help. It is easy and common in our society to be so wrapped up in ourselves (and our electronics!) that we don't even see others. Similarly, it is easy to see someone with a visible problem as somehow inferior, perhaps having caused their own problem. To look at someone and see the light of the creator and show kindness in the manner we ourselves would like to receive outweighs many, many wrongs. These acts bring balance and stability to the world.

Smiling and thanking the cashier or bus driver may take less than 20 seconds, but it changes the world.

DAY
17

If I am not for myself,
who is for me?

Confidence is often misunderstood. There needs to be a certain amount of confidence for a person to take action. We cannot be constantly doing and undoing, deciding to act and, in the next minute, deciding not to act. Decisiveness and confidence go hand and hand. Confidence takes knowledge of resources, inner and outer, into account. Confidence is based on the certainty that the Creator intends for us to fulfill our purpose. This is not arrogance because arrogance neither looks to the Creator nor depends on resources beyond human ability.

Additionally, the world around us expects us to signal who we are. If we are "comfortable in our own skin," peaceful and confident in who we are, we bring peace with us. We signal trustworthiness. The world is for us.

A fundamental lack of confidence is basically an argument with the Creator. Here we are in a beautiful world, yet we ourselves are a mistake.

If I am not for myself, perhaps I need to sit down and have a heart to heart talk with myself. No one is exactly like me. I am not replaceable. I may or may not feel I know my purpose, but one thing is certain. No one else can fulfill my purpose.

DAY
18

If I am only for myself, what am I?

I was pleased to discover that trees communicate. They may not have community that we understand, but they nevertheless share knowledge. There are many types of societies in the animal world. The social intelligence of ants and bees as well as the pack behavior of wolves have parallels with humanity. However, there is a deep lesson in the fact that, for us, considerateness is a choice. We could choose to separate ourselves from community. The problem with this choice is that an essential component of our identity is in community.

How we treat others reveals our heart. How we see others reveals our consciousness. When we separate from community, we block a unique window on who we are.

DAY
19

If not now, when?

Generally, there is no better time to start something than the present moment. If we don't start something now, at least get it on the calendar. Schedule it now! Of course, as the sages pointed out, we don't always finish our good work, but at least we don't turn away from it. There is some presumption in postponing a good deed. Why do we think we are promised tomorrow?

There is some action in the direction of good that we can do in the next five minutes.

How much energy and opportunity is squandered waiting for a perfect time?

Hillel confronts us with the need to bring our values into the present. He calls us across the millennia, "What are you waiting for?"

DAY
20

**Provide thyself
with a teacher.**

There are areas of mastery we cannot approach without instruction and correction. We invest in a teacher who has mastered what we seek to learn.

Years ago, I stood on the serving line of a tennis court with a tennis instructor correcting my serve. On the next court over was a man with a bucket of balls working on his serve, which was erratic. As he hit ball after ball, he became consistent. It was not a good serve, but it was consistent. My instructor observed, "Practice does not make perfect; practice makes permanent." Without a teacher, our poor habits become ingrained. We don't even know it. It seemed my tennis neighbor walked off the court pleased with himself. He had worked on his serve. Without a teacher, it is easy to deceive ourselves about our progress.

Teachability or correctability is a hallmark of wisdom. Without a teacher, we are unlikely to recognize if we are teachable or not. Without teachers, most of us are blind to our mistakes.

Often a teacher shows us a path to knowledge we would not have seen on our own.

DAY
21

**And possess thyself
of a companion.**

A companion that we learn with stimulates us to grapple with hard concepts. We are forced to express what we are discovering.

As Francis Bacon said, "Reading maketh a full man; conference, a ready man; and writing, an exact man." It takes a process to arrive at clarity of thought. We can study, but sharing with colleagues brings what we've studied into our awareness.

Of course, the goal is accurate thinking, but we need to perceive the ideas before we can sort them. As we share our thoughts, they become more precise and amplified. Sometimes just sharing improves our clarity. Sometimes our companion's comments reveal weak conclusions. Sometimes expressing it to a friend takes us to a level where we can bring it to our teacher. Correction is most helpful to a student who is ready.

DAY
22

Do not separate thyself
from the congregation.

There is illusion that we can progress in isolation. This is the proverbial hermit on top of the mountain. The hermit is a wise spiritual being who has made great advances in isolation. There are several problems with this picture. One problem is we all have "blind spots." Community protects us with repeated opportunities to give. For me, however, the major problem is that connection with the Creator and with one another is the essence of spirituality. Being part of community, moreover, is not just about personal benefit. We each have gifts that no one else brings. In a certain sense, our gifts don't belong to us. Rather, they belong to those who receive them through us. Some of our gifts may not be obvious to us but are so valuable in community. For example, perhaps we have lost a parent, and that may cause us to have insight and compassion as we sit with someone who is just now experiencing that transition.

Hillel's guidance can keep us from disconnection and help us be part of a greater sense of identity and purpose.

DAY
23

There are four kinds of temper: he whom is easy to provoke and easy to pacify, his loss disappears in his gain . . .

There are three reasons for an easy-to-anger and easy-to-forgive attitude.

First, there are those who have an "easy-come, easy-go" mentality. Nothing seems too heavy to them. Generally, they lack revelation that life has meaning. Some part of their soul remains asleep. They partly awaken when there is an event. The unexpected, adverse, unwanted negative shakes them awake. Then they come to themselves and think, "No big deal."

Second, there are those who have a sunny disposition. They are easily irritated, but their default feeling is happiness. Their habit of happiness keeps them from bearing a grudge.

Third, there are those who are perfectionists, who are easily irritated by imperfection but have thought it through. They are self-aware and have decided in advance not to stay angry. As they develop further, they will become less easily angered and move into a more evolved state.

DAY
24

He whom it is hard
to provoke and hard
to pacify, his gain
disappears in his loss.

This type of person shows up when life is favorable; we are well-rested, so we are not irritable. Then something outrageous and unjust happens to us. That event finally provokes us, and we cannot let it go. We tell friends and acquaintances. We see our life as injured and maintain the injury as evidence against the wrong doer, evidence we need to preserve so we can always exact justice.

In one way, this is spiritual paralysis. We are "stuck in a rut" of rehearsing an injury. The injury is proof of how wronged we have been. Therefore, if we heal from it, we will not receive the justice that we believe is due. If this process continues, we refuse to consider the positive inside the negative. If we look back on the lessons of life, some things that looked negative turned out to be very positive. Choosing to have a certainty in the goodness of the Creator can free us to forgive. In other words, if we believe that there will be a good outcome, eventually we can move forward. The moment we forgive, we are freed from the past. Once out of a negative cycle, we can move forward on a positive path. Justice is in the hands of the one True Judge.

DAY
25

He whom it is hard
to provoke and easy
to pacify is a saint.

A righteous person has enough confidence in the truth to overlook an insult. Commitment to living the truth requires taking responsibility for feelings. I see patience as a spiritual force that works together with certainty in the Light of the Creator to give us the reserve to "ride out" difficulty and suffering. Spiritual decisions pretty much have to be made in advance. You can decide to be that person who is easily pacified.

To not forgive easily inevitably leads to bitterness and, as has been said, being bitter is like drinking poison and expecting the other person to die.

It is not necessary to have a genuine apology to forgive. We would naturally forgive a child or a person of limited capacity. We just clean up the "spilled milk" and move on. Why would we leave the spilled milk on the floor and wait for a two-year-old to get the revelation and ability to clean it up? It could take years.

There are people who do terrible things. They lack awareness and aren't open to instruction. We clean up the mess as best we can and set up boundaries for the future. Sometimes we have been the people who have done the terrible things. We clean up the mess as best we can, forgiving our "two-year-old" self. We base this not on merit but on a decision to show love.

DAY
26

He whom it is easy to provoke and hard to pacify is a wicked man.

There are days when we are overwhelmed and irritable. Days when we are not ready for an adverse event are often spoiled after that event when we fester all day about how wrong it was. We could be correct that the event was provocative, but perhaps we could have avoided being provoked by perceiving it differently. Perhaps we could have chosen to be pacified right away. To forgive because the life we have right now—our next breath of air—is proof we have been forgiven.

What does it mean to be "wicked"? In one sense, it is consistently choosing a path based on deception. It is developing habits that lead to an unfulfilled life. The "wicked" do not share their gifts, talents, or energy with the world. Selfishness and stinginess lead to being easily offended. Acting on kindness, generosity, and compassion changes this. One generous action moves us away from poor choices.

DAY
27

It is not thy duty to complete the work.

S ometimes darkness seems very great. The task seems overwhelming. If we were tasked with bringing light to the whole world perhaps we could never get past the planning stage. Our task is sharing whatever good we have right now, where we are.

DAY
28

**But neither art thou
free to desist from it.**

Just because we cannot rid the world of darkness does not release us from the duty to share our light. We often respond to feeling overwhelmed with a desire to quit, but there is always a lie in abandoning one's purpose. The lie is that right now doesn't matter, that what we are doing right now has no meaning. Here's the truth: we all desire meaning. We all require purpose in life. Sometimes purpose is expressed in social sharing, sometimes in creating something of beauty. But purpose demands expression, and in expressing purpose, we affirm our identity; we experience fulfillment. We are born as vessels that channel the Light of the Creator. We are never free from the desire to share light. Awe and respect for the Creator and recognition of the purpose we have as sharers of light lead to deep satisfaction.

DAY
29

Let thy friend's honor
be as dear to thee
as thine own.

We live in a society where "put downs" are considered humorous. A joke can place a companion in a bad light. We may be silent when an absent friend is criticized. Sometimes a friend is unpopular for a season. And it may be unfair, unjust. And it may be awkward and difficult to defend them. If we were in their place, would we want someone to defend us?

DAY
30

Say not anything which cannot be understood at once.

am choosing to end this month of thinking with a plea for restraint and clarity of speech. Restricting speech to words that bring light right now is powerful.

The first step is to recognize words are important. Words crystalize our thoughts, and thoughts both originate and reinforce our speech. Our lives are directed by those words. Skilled communication brings connection. Connection is the basis of mutual respect. Mutual respect is the foundation of peace.

The second step is to recognize silence is important. In fact, companionable silence is a form of connection. It is a ground of connection on which simple clear words of light bring life to ourselves and our companions.

Suppose we end this month by pausing before we speak. Enjoy a companionable silence, and choose words that are mutually understandable. Beware however that we do not reduce complex thoughts to simplistic slogans. Instead, let us become seekers of wisdom who peacefully consider differing views while maintaining our determination to dwell together in unity.

"Hinei Ma Tov" is a song from Psalm 133 that we sing on Friday nights. It tells of the goodness and pleasantness that spreads heart to heart when we choose to get along, when we live and work together hand to hand.

May you have more of this pleasantness and goodness in your life—day after day.

About the Author

DR. CURRIER lives a quiet life in a little brick rambler in Virginia. Besides the oak trees that surround her, the nearest companions are her two dogs. They constantly encourage her to pay attention. She has been on a journey to understand health and wisdom for over fifty years and has enjoyed every minute along the way.